IMMIGRATION

by John Wood

BookLife
PUBLISHING

©2018
BookLife Publishing
King's Lynn
Norfolk PE30 4LS

A catalogue record for this
book is available from the
British Library.

ISBN: 978-1-78637-426-4

Written by:
John Wood

Edited by:
Robin Twiddy

Designed by:
Dan Scase

APPROVED

PHOTO CREDITS

CONTENTS

Words that look like **THIS** are explained in the glossary on page 31.

WHAT IS IMMIGRATION?

When people go to live in another country, it is called migration. Immigration is when people come into a country – these people are known as immigrants. Emigration is when people leave a country – these people are called emigrants.

Morocco
Tunisia
Algeria
Libya
Egypt
Mauritania
Mali
Niger
Chad
Sudan
Eritrea
Senegal
The Gambia
Guinea-Bissau
Burkina Faso
Benin
Djibouti
Guinea
Sierra Leone
Cote d'Ivoire
Togo
Nigeria
Liberia
Ghana
Cameroon
EMIGRATION
South Sudan
Ethiopia
Equatorial Guinea
Republic of the Congo
Uganda
Somalia
IMMIGRATION
Gabon
Democratic Republic of the Congo
Rwanda
Burundi
Kenya
Tanzania
Angola
Malawi
Zambia
Mozambique
Madagascar
Zimbabwe
Namibia
Botswana
Swaziland
South Africa

Immigrating is not like having a holiday. Immigrants stay in a new country to live, work and go to school. Immigrants are very important, and they are a big part of a country, the same as everyone else.

All around the world, over 244 million people have moved and now live in a new country.

The US takes in the most immigrants in the world. However, The United Arab Emirates has the largest number of immigrants compared to non-immigrants of any country.

4

IMMIGRATION IN HISTORY

Humans have always moved to new places.

Humans have always immigrated to new countries. It is thought that the first humans probably came from somewhere in Africa. Over time, humans spread out all over the world. Now we live all over the place, on almost every continent.

If most people looked far enough back in their **FAMILY TREE**, they would probably find an **ANCESTOR** who immigrated to the country they now live in. Countries like the UK have a long and interesting history of people coming from all over the world to live.

Lots of different people have lived in Britain throughout history, from the Romans to the Vikings.

WHY DO PEOPLE IMMIGRATE?

REASONS TO MOVE

Some people need to immigrate because they have a new job in a new country. Others might have family that live in a different country and they want to be near to them.

Some people move so that they can go to a certain school or university.

Things that make people want to leave their country are sometimes called push factors. Things that make people want to be part of another country are sometimes called pull factors.

CULTURE

Culture is a word used to describe the way of life for a large group of people. A culture is made up of lots of things, like **TRADITIONS**, food, clothes, art and ideas about how life should be lived. Sometimes people move to a new country because they love the culture of that country, and they want to be a part of it.

Traditional celebrations are part of culture. This celebration, called Holi, is held in India every year to celebrate the arrival of spring and the victory of good over evil.

THEY DON'T LIKE THE COUNTRY THEY ARE IN

TO FIND SOMEWHERE SAFE

Many people move away because they don't feel there are any OPPORTUNITIES in the country they were born in. Their country might have rules that make them feel trapped or ignored. They might think they will have a better life in a different place.

Some people live in dangerous countries. There may be NATURAL DISASTERS, war, lots of crime or a dangerous government. They might want to migrate to a country that feels safer.

For example, people might feel that they are not allowed to speak their mind in their home country.

CRIME SCENE DO NOT CROSS   CRIME SCENE DO NOT CROSS   CRIME SCENE DO NOT CROSS

CRIME SCENE

7

LIFE AS AN IMMIGRANT

LANGUAGE

After arriving in a new country, an immigrant might need to learn a new language. Learning a new language can be hard. Even if someone can speak a language, it might still be difficult to understand others, and make themselves understood.

A NEW WAY OF LIFE

Life can be very exciting for an immigrant. There might be new things to try every day, and new places to explore. Some immigrants see moving to a different country as an adventure.

GETTING USED TO CULTURE

A new culture can take time to get used to. In some cultures, people are loud and show their emotions, while in others people are quieter. People work very long hours in some countries, but in other countries they are more relaxed.

In some countries, people drive on the left. In other countries, people drive on the right. This is an important thing to get used to.

In some parts of Europe, people can work up to 42.3 hours a week. In other European countries, like Slovenia, people work around 39.3 hours a week. This might take a while to get used to.

BEING MISTREATED

Unfortunately, when people look or sound different to everyone else, they are sometimes bullied. People can say horrible and unfair things to people who have immigrated. They might mistrust them, or tell them to go back to their own country. This is wrong because a person who has immigrated belongs in the country as much as anyone else.

Bullying can make someone feel very alone and unwanted. This can make immigration difficult and unpleasant.

9

HOW IS IMMIGRATION HELPFUL?

DOCTORS AND NURSES

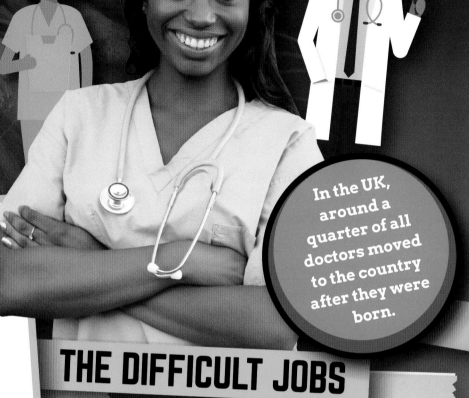

When a country takes in people from all over the world, it can be very helpful for everyone. A lot of immigrants are very clever and educated, and able to do important jobs. For example, many immigrants are doctors, scientists and **COMPUTER PROGRAMMERS**. Without immigrants, countries wouldn't have enough people to do these jobs.

In the UK, around a quarter of all doctors moved to the country after they were born.

THE DIFFICULT JOBS

Jobs like cleaning or picking vegetables are difficult but low-paid.

Immigrants also do essential but difficult jobs, such as farming, cleaning and service jobs, that many people don't want to do. Although these jobs are often low-paid, they help immigrants to earn money when they begin their life in a new country. Countries that don't allow many immigrants in have trouble finding people to do difficult low-paid jobs. For example, Japan only allows a few highly educated immigrants in. Japan's difficult jobs need to be done by other members of SOCIETY, like elderly people.

MORE MONEY

When people live in a country, they spend money on lots of things. They buy things from shops, go to restaurants and use SERVICES like buses and trains. Their money flows around the country, making other people richer. This means that immigrants bring lots of money to a country just by living there.

Shops might make less money if there were no immigrants.

TAXES

Adults pay taxes. Taxes are when the government takes a bit of money from everyone to pay for things like roads, HEALTHCARE and police officers. Immigrants pay taxes too, which helps the country pay for these important things.

Taxes pay for many jobs. For example, taxes pay for people to come and take rubbish and recycling away.

SHARING CULTURE

When people from different countries come together, they can create a mix of culture. Areas with lots of different cultures are vibrant and exciting. People can learn a lot by sharing cultures, and new things can be created.

What is part of your culture?

FOOD

CHICKEN TIKKA MASALA

Many cultures have shared recipes and food. Britain is a good example of this. Indian curries are very popular in Britain. New Indian-like curries have been invented in Britain, such as chicken tikka masala. This is thanks to Indian immigrants sharing their culture with British people.

CLOTHES

When different cultures come together, people have the opportunity to dress differently and mix styles. Clothes are an important way of showing who we are.

CELEBRATIONS

Different cultures and religions have different holidays. When a city is full of people from different cultures, there are lots of celebrations. There may be fireworks, decorations and celebrations in the street throughout the year.

ART

Different cultures can come together and create new art, such as films, music and books. For example, jazz is a type of music that came from mixing music and ideas from Africa and Europe.

13

ENCLAVES

When a lot of people from the same country immigrate together, they sometimes make an enclave. An enclave is an area of a city or country with a lot of people and CHARACTERISTICS from somewhere else. Some enclaves can feel a bit separate from the rest of the country.

In some enclaves, the people might speak a separate language and have a different culture to the country that they live in.

Enclaves can help immigrants cope with moving to a new country. An enclave can remind them of home. It might be easier for people to find jobs, friends and advice in an enclave.

This is an Indian enclave of Singapore called Little India.

14

CHINATOWN

There are many Chinese enclaves all over the world. The enclaves are named Chinatown, and they have become famous. Many road signs and shop names are in Chinese. Some people think that enclaves can add an exciting, different type of culture to a city.

The Chinatown in Manhattan is one of the oldest and largest enclaves in the world. It is also thought to have the largest Chinese population outside of Asia.

BRITISH ENCLAVES IN SPAIN

There are many British enclaves in Spain. The signs are in English, not Spanish, because many people who live there don't speak Spanish. British food is sold there, like pie, or fish and chips. Some people think that enclaves can make it harder for people to truly become a part of another country.

This is Orihuela Costa, the biggest British enclave in Spain.

MIGRANTS IN HISTORY & MIGRANTS TODAY

History is full of big migrations. Moving to another country was dangerous 100 years ago, and it can still be dangerous for some people now, but people still do it to find a better future.

EXAMPLE: THE UNITED STATES OF AMERICA

Immigration has played an important part of the history of the US, and it is still an important issue today. Aside from the INDIGENOUS (say: in-dij-in-uss) people who lived there first, most other people come from families that immigrated to the country. The US is sometimes called a 'melting pot', which means it is a huge mix of different people and cultures. 'The American Dream' is an important idea in the US – it is the idea that anyone can come and be successful if they work hard. Lots of people come to the US to work hard and be successful.

This is The Statue of Liberty, in New York, US. It is a symbol for freedom and fairness.

IMMIGRATION IN THE FUTURE

Immigration is becoming more and more widespread. There could be many reasons for this. For example, transport is a lot better now than it has been before in history. This means that getting around the world is easier and cheaper.

Before modern transport, migration was often dangerous. Some migration is still dangerous (see pages 20–21 and 26–27).

The UN has found that 2.8% of people in the world were migrants in 2000. However, now 3.4% of the people in the world are migrants.

The world is a lot more connected now. Countries all over the world trade with each other. The internet allows people from all around the world to read about different countries and cultures. This means there are more reasons to move to a different country, for example to work or to be part of a culture you love.

BECOMING A CITIZEN

WHAT IS A CITIZEN?

When someone **LEGALLY** belongs to a country, they are called a citizen of that country. Becoming a citizen is also called getting citizenship.

People are **AUTOMATICALLY** a citizen of the country they were born in, but they can also become citizens of other countries.

IMMIGRANTS WHO ARE NOT CITIZENS

The rules are different for every country, but immigrants usually have to have lots of paperwork and reasons to remain in a country. For example, they often need a travel visa, which is a card that proves they are allowed to stay.

PASSPORT

Visitor Visa
Application
a temporary stay in co
for?
Business

Some immigrants are only allowed to stay because of things like work or school. If anything about their situation changes, or if the laws about immigration change, they might be forced to leave.

PASSPORT

REASONS TO BE A CITIZEN

There are lots of reasons to become a citizen, such as:
- Being able to vote in elections
- Not having to pay to update visa documents
- Always being allowed to stay
- Able to apply for more jobs
- Easier to travel because citizens get a passport

Some people take part in a **CEREMONY** to mark their citizenship.

VOTE

HOW TO BECOME A CITIZEN

To become a citizen, immigrants must get in touch with the government and apply for citizenship. If they have the right paperwork, they usually take an exam. If they pass this exam, they legally become a citizen.

Some people become citizens because they feel proud of the country that they live in, and want to be part of it legally.

ASYLUM AND IMMIGRATION

WHAT IS ASYLUM?

Asylum is when someone is being protected in another country because it was not safe to stay in their own. People who are leaving their country for protection are called refugees, or sometimes asylum seekers.

Universal Declaration of Human Rights

Asylum is a basic **HUMAN RIGHT.** Every country should look after refugees who are trying to get away from danger.

REFUGEES

Refugees often come from countries that are at war, or have dangerous governments. Refugees often have to travel illegally in order to quickly get to safety. This can be dangerous. Many refugees have seen loved ones die because of the dangerous situations they have been in.

Many refugees have been through extremely hard times.

REFUGEES AND IMMIGRANTS AROUND THE WORLD

Countries around the world have different views about taking in people from other countries. In 2017, the President of the United States, Donald Trump, passed laws to stop many refugees and immigrants coming into the country. This affected people coming from countries like Iraq, Syria, Iran and Libya.

REFUGEES & IMMIGRANTS ARE WELCOME HERE

There were many protests around the US to show that the people wanted to welcome refugees and immigrants.

The Prime Minister of Canada, Justin Trudeau, sent a message to immigrants and refugees around the world saying that they were welcome in Canada.

PRIME MINISTER TRUDEAU

FAMOUS IMMIGRANTS

There are many famous people who have immigrated to a different country. Immigration helped them be the best they could be, and helped them create and do things that benefited the world.

ALBERT EINSTEIN

Albert Einstein was a famous scientist who came up with many important theories. When he was sixteen, he immigrated to Switzerland because he didn't like how he was taught in his home country, Germany. He did most of his important work in Switzerland. When World War II was about to begin, Einstein immigrated again to the US.

Einstein's work has helped us understand a lot about how the universe works.

ELON MUSK

Elon Musk is a businessman who was born in South Africa. He moved to Canada when he was 17. He then moved to the US after leaving university a few years later. He founded lots of companies, and now makes things like electric cars, super-fast transport, and space rockets.

Elon Musk's companies could help us explore space and save the environment.

MO FARAH

Mo Farah was born in Somalia, but moved to England when he was eight years old. He left Somalia to escape a **CIVIL WAR**. Since immigrating, Mo Farah has become one of the best British runners of all time.

MO FARAH, AT THE LONDON OLYMPICS

NATALIE PORTMAN

Natalie Portman was born in Israel. When she was a young child, she moved to the US. Natalie Portman is now a famous model and actress. If she hadn't immigrated to the US, she might not have had the opportunity to become a great actress.

NATALIE PORTMAN HAS BEEN IN FILMS SUCH AS THOR, STAR WARS AND BLACK SWAN.

SERGEY BRIN

Sergey Brin, a **JEWISH** man who was born in Russia, moved to the US. He and his family moved because people were being **VIOLENT** towards Jewish people in Russia at the time. At university, Sergey Brin met Larry Page, and they created Google.

Sometimes, extremely important inventions and ideas like Google are only possible because of immigration and the sharing of ideas.

24

ELIZABETH STERN

Elizabeth Stern was an important doctor and scientist. She was born in Canada, but moved to California, US in 1963. Elizabeth Stern studied a serious illness called cancer. Her work made it easier to find cancer as early as possible. This saved many lives.

This is Los Angeles, a city in California where Elizabeth Stern did most of her research.

INDRA NOOYI

Indra Nooyi was born in India. She moved to the US to go to a business school. Indra Nooyi is now in charge of PepsiCo, which is an extremely successful food and drinks company in America.

PepsiCo creates lots of jobs and money for America.

CONTROLLING MOVEMENT

Each country has its own rules about immigration. Unless they are a refugee, people are not allowed to move to a country without PERMISSION. They might get permission to come for a few years, or they might get permission to live there forever. Countries have many ways to control immigration.

PASSPORTS AND EXIT CHECKS

Before you enter or leave a country, most of the time there will be people who check your passport and make a note of where you are going and how long you will be there.

A passport is a small booklet with important information which gets stamped when you move through different countries.

PAPERWORK

Immigrants have lots of paperwork that they need to keep updated. When applying for things like jobs or homes, immigrants have to show their paperwork. If something is wrong or outdated, then they may be refused.

In the US, a green card lets a person work and live in the US forever.

BORDER AGENCY

Many countries have a special group of people who are in charge of controlling immigration. This is usually called a border agency. They check paperwork, and record who is moving in and out of the country. These agencies are controlled by the government agencies, just like the police are.

In the US, immigration is controlled by Border Patrol, also called Border Police.

ILLEGAL IMMIGRATION

When someone moves to a country that they do not have permission to be in, this is called illegal immigration. If they are running away from danger, they are called refugees.

Countries often put up fences and have border agencies to stop illegal immigrants.

WHY DOES ILLEGAL IMMIGRATION HAPPEN?

Illegal immigrants move into countries because they want a better future for themselves. Even if their own country isn't dangerous, it might still be very hard to live there. If they do not get permission, but are desperate to move, they might think they have no other option but to move illegally.

Moving to a country illegally can be expensive and dangerous.

WHAT HAPPENS TO PEOPLE WHO MOVE ILLEGALLY?

When a border agency finds illegal immigrants, they may arrest them or put them in jail for up to 48 hours. After this, the government will usually try and DEPORT the person who has immigrated illegally.

A person can appeal against being deported – this means they can argue that they have a right to stay.

Some illegal immigrants are treated very badly.

Immigration needs to be legal because the government needs to know who is living in the country, and keep a record of who they are and what they do. It is important to remember that every person – whether they are a citizen or an illegal immigrant – has a right to be treated fairly and with dignity.

ACTIVITY

Here are some questions and activities for you and the rest of your class.

Do you know anyone who has immigrated? Maybe you could write about their story. You could draw pictures to show what happened.

Can you list three reasons why people might immigrate?

Can you think of three things you like about other cultures? Think about food, films and holidays.

GLOSSARY

ANCESTOR	person from whom one is descended, for example a great-grandparent
AUTOMATICALLY	without conscious thought or control
CEREMONY	a special event performed on a religious or social occasion
CHARACTERISTICS	features of a thing that help to identify it
CIVIL WAR	fighting between different groups of people in the same country
COMPUTER PROGRAMMERS	people who write programs for a computer
DEPORT	force someone to leave a country, usually because they have broken the law
FAMILY TREE	a diagram that shows the history of a family, and all the members that have come before
HEALTHCARE	a system which is set up by a country so that people are looked after when they get ill
HUMAN RIGHT	an entitlement to do or have something that every person should have
INDIGENOUS	originating or naturally found in a particular place
JEWISH	a person who follows the religion called Judaism
LEGALLY	performed within the limits of the law
NATURAL DISASTERS	natural events that cause great damage to an area
OPPORTUNITIES	chances to do something, often positive
PERMISSION	when someone in charge says someone is allowed to do something
SERVICES	jobs that someone is paid to do which do not involve any physical goods being exchanged
SOCIETY	a collection of people living together
TRADITIONS	related to very old behaviours or belief
VIOLENT	use force to physically hurt someone

INDEX